How Your
BODY
Works

Your
Digestive
System

How Your **BODY** Works

Your Digestive System

Anita Ganeri

Gareth Stevens Publishing

A WORLD ALMANAC EDUCATION GROUP COMPANY

ACKNOWLEDGMENTS
With thanks to: Kelsey Sharman, Thomas Keen, Matthew Botterill, Ashley Richardson, Charmaine Francis-Sammon, Courtney Thomas, Lily Dang, Frankie Iszard, Imran Akhtar, Justin Mooi, Indiana Frankham.
Models from Truly Scrumptious Ltd.

Please visit our web site at: www.garethstevens.com
For a free color catalog describing Gareth Stevens Publishing's
list of high-quality books and multimedia programs, call
1-800-542-2595 (USA) or 1-800-387-3178 (Canada).
Gareth Stevens Publishing's fax: (414) 332-3567.

Library of Congress Cataloging-in-Publication Data available upon request from publisher.
Fax (414) 336-0157 for the attention of the Publishing Records Department.

ISBN 0-8368-3633-2

This North American edition first published in 2003 by
Gareth Stevens Publishing
A World Almanac Education Group Company
330 West Olive Street, Suite 100
Milwaukee, WI 53212 USA

Original edition © 2003 by Evans Brothers Limited. First published in 2003 by Evans Brothers Limited, 2A Portman Mansions, Chiltern Street, London W1U 6NR, United Kingdom. This U.S. edition published under license from Evans Brothers Limited. This U.S. edition © 2003 by Gareth Stevens, Inc. Additional end matter © 2003 by Gareth Stevens, Inc.

Designer: Mark Holt
Artwork: Julian Baker
Photography: Steve Shott
Consultant: Dr. M. Turner

Gareth Stevens Editor: Carol Ryback
Gareth Stevens Designer: Katherine A. Goedheer

Photo credits:
Science Photo Library: Omikron, page 10; John Burbidge, page 12; Quest, page 16; CAMR/A. B. Dowsett, page 19; Manfred Kage, page 21; BSIP VEM, page 23.

Printed in the United States of America

1 2 3 4 5 6 7 8 9 07 06 05 04 03

Contents

Why Do You Eat?

Feeling hungry? **Hunger** is your body's way of telling you it needs food. Food has **nutrients**, **vitamins**, and **minerals** in it that your body uses to grow, stay healthy, and mend itself. Your food also gives you **energy**. You feel hungry when your energy supply runs low.

Amazing!

You eat an amazing 33 tons (30 tonnes) of food in your life — that's the weight of six elephants!

Your food tube is coiled up to fit inside your body. Its actual length is about 30 feet (9 meters).

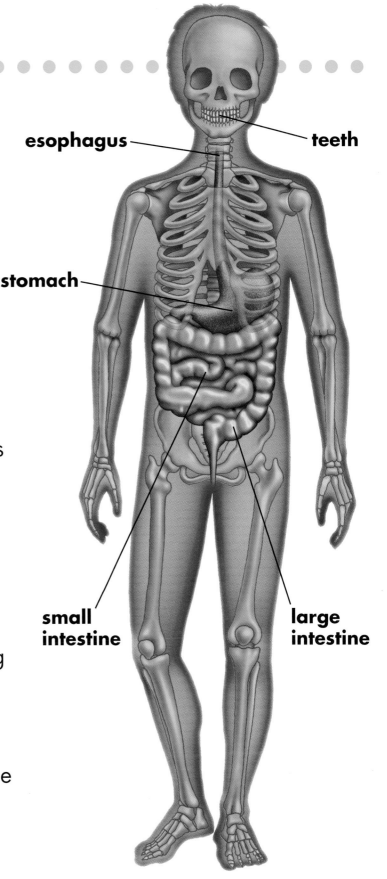

esophagus

teeth

stomach

small intestine

large intestine

When you eat a piece of yummy pizza, where does it go? Your body cannot use a piece of pizza the way it looks when you eat it. The pizza must be broken down by your body into pieces small enough to pass into your blood. Your blood carries the pieces of food all around your body for energy. The process of turning food into energy is called **digestion**. Food gets digested as it travels through your food tube. Your food tube goes all the way from your mouth to your bottom.

7

Chomping and Chewing

Digestion begins in your mouth. With your first bite, your teeth start breaking down your food by chewing it into smaller pieces. Your tongue helps by pushing the food around your mouth. Your mouth also makes a watery spit called **saliva**. Your saliva wets the food so it becomes slippery and easy to swallow. That's why a delicious meal makes your mouth water.

Amazing!

Tooth **enamel** is the hardest part of your body — even harder than your bones.

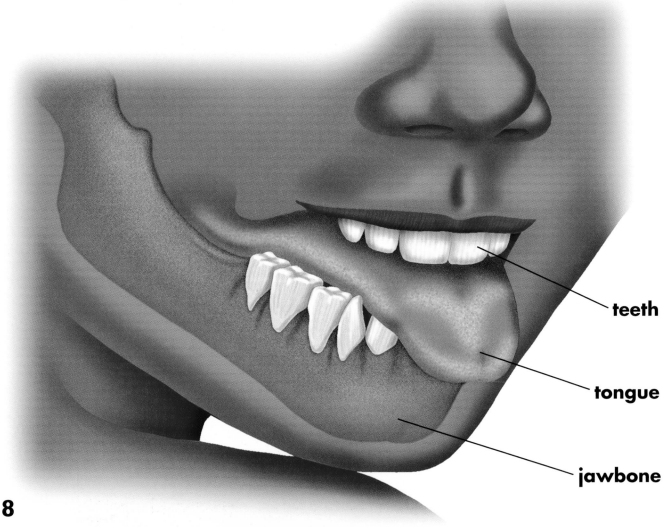

teeth

tongue

jawbone

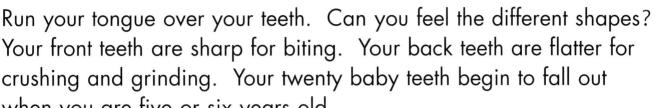

Run your tongue over your teeth. Can you feel the different shapes? Your front teeth are sharp for biting. Your back teeth are flatter for crushing and grinding. Your twenty baby teeth begin to fall out when you are five or six years old.
Soon, thirty-two bigger teeth will grow in their place.

Tiny pieces of food can stick between your teeth when you eat. Brush your teeth daily to keep them clean.

How Does It Taste?

You taste your food with your tongue. Look at your tongue in a mirror. It is covered with tiny bumps that hold your **taste buds**. Your taste buds send messages along **nerves** to your brain so you know what your food tastes like. Taste buds on different areas of your tongue taste sweet, sour, salty, and bitter flavors. Tasting is very useful. It tells you if food is good or if it's spoiled.

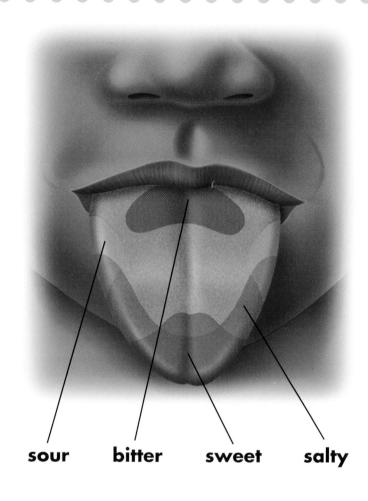

sour   **bitter**   **sweet**   **salty**

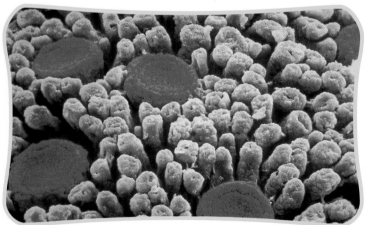

The larger, flat bumps on your tongue hold taste buds.

Amazing!

You have more than 10,000 taste buds on your tongue. Some of them stop working as you get older.

When your nose is blocked up because of a cold, you probably think your food doesn't have much taste. That's because your sense of smell helps you taste your food.

When the food you eat has a strong taste, such as a sour lemon, you might make a funny face.

Swallowing

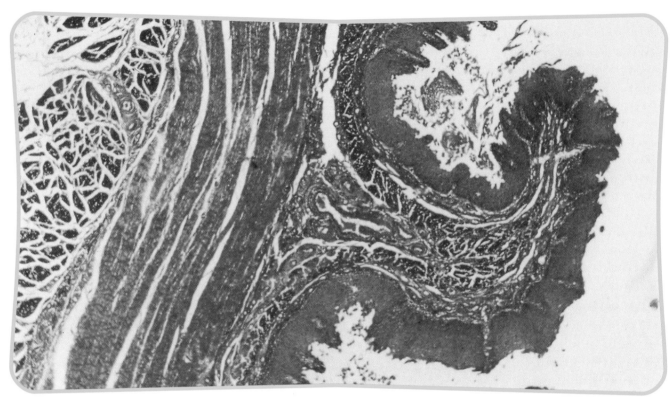

Muscles in the wall of your esophagus push food toward your **stomach**.

After you have chewed your food, your tongue pushes it to the back of your mouth so you can swallow it. The food you swallow enters a food tube called your **esophagus**. Your esophagus leads to your stomach. But the food does not simply slide down your esophagus to your stomach. Your esophagus is lined with muscles that squeeze to push the food along.

Amazing!

In one day, you swallow about 3,000 times. Gulp!

Your esophagus is next to your **windpipe** in your throat. You use your esophagus for swallowing. You use your windpipe for breathing. Usually, a tiny flap covers the top of your windpipe when you swallow. Sometimes, your food goes down the "wrong way" and into your windpipe instead of your esophagus, and you **choke**.

The food you eat squeezes down your esophagus the way toothpaste squeezes out of a tube.

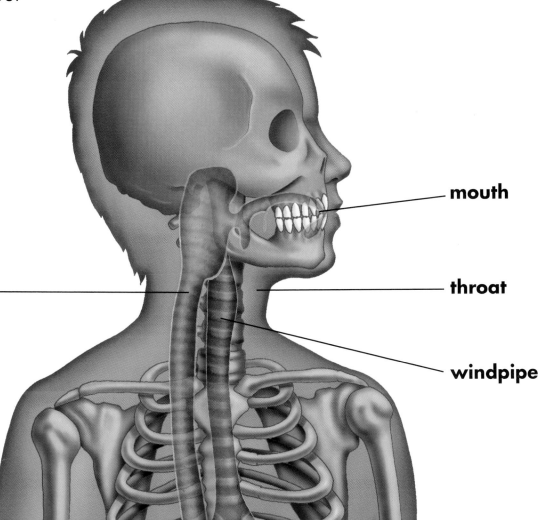

mouth

esophagus

throat

windpipe

Inside Your Stomach

Your esophagus squeezes your food into your stomach. Your stomach is a thick, stretchy bag made of strong muscles. It mashes and squashes your food up even more and pours special juices on your food to break it down. Your stomach juices also help kill any harmful **germs** in your food that might cause a stomachache. By the time your food leaves your stomach, it looks like a thick soup.

Amazing!

A meal stays in your stomach for about four hours. It takes about three days to travel all the way through you.

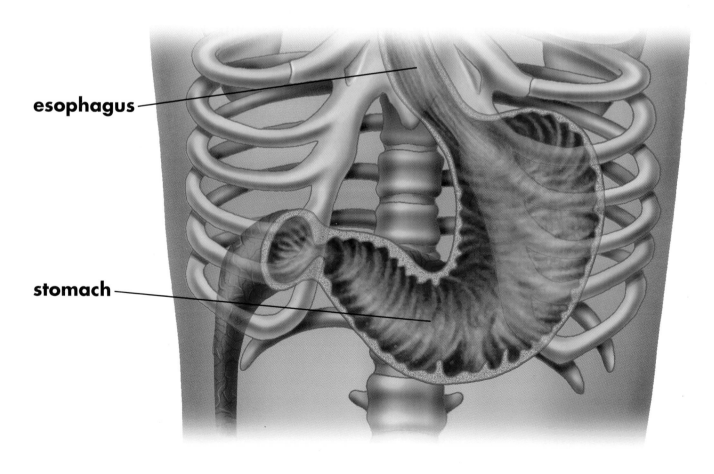

esophagus

stomach

Your stomach gets bigger as it fills up with food. When your stomach gets full, it sends messages to your brain so you stop eating. If you eat too much, or if you eat food that is spoiled, you might get sick. Then, your stomach muscles will force your food back up.

Does your stomach growl when you feel hungry? The noise is made by air inside your stomach being squished and squeezed.

A Long Journey

Next, the thick soupy mixture of your food squeezes from your stomach into your **small intestine**. Your small intestine is very long, but it is coiled up tightly to fit inside you. Your small intestine also makes juices to digest your food even further. The nutrients from your food can now seep through the sides of your small intestine into your blood. Your blood carries the nutrients around your body to give you energy.

Amazing!

Your small intestine is an amazing 13 feet (4 meters) long. It's called small because it's less than 2 inches (4 centimeters) wide.

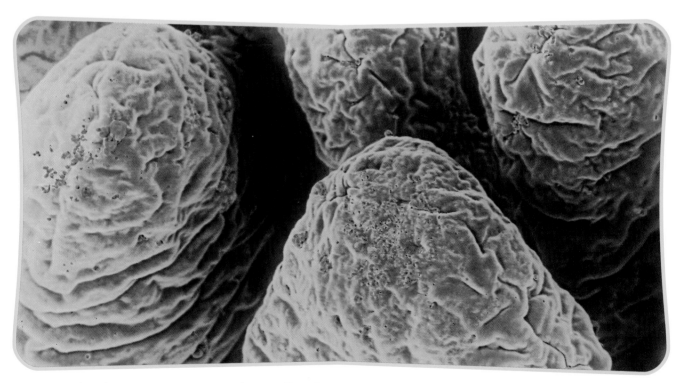

Under a microscope, the walls of your small intestine look like a towel.

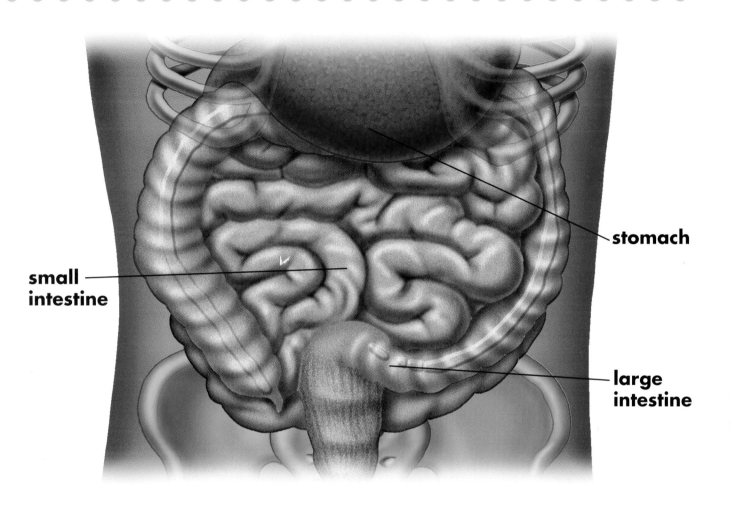

small intestine

stomach

large intestine

After you eat, your body works on digesting your food instead of working your muscles. Hard exercise after meals can cause a muscle **cramp**.

Food that your body can't use gets pushed from your small intestine into your **large intestine**. Your large intestine is much shorter and wider than your small intestine. Your large intestine forms your waste food into a soft lump and stores it until you go to the bathroom.

Your Liver and Pancreas

Your blood passes the digested food through your **liver**. Your liver does some important jobs in the digestion of your food. Your liver removes and stores the nutrients from your food until your body can use them. Your liver also cleans any **poisons** from your food so that they do not harm you. Then your blood takes the good parts of your food to the rest of your body.

Your liver is on the right side of your body, just in front of and level with your stomach.

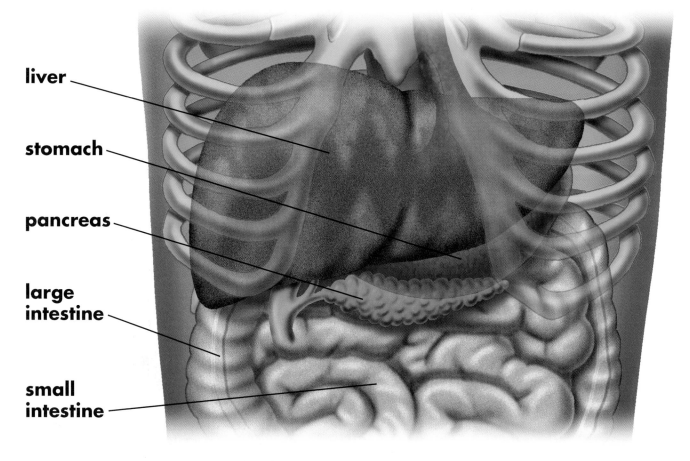

liver

stomach

pancreas

large intestine

small intestine

Your liver makes a green juice called **bile**. Bile helps break up the fat in your food. A small bag, called your **gall bladder**, stores the bile. Then your bile flows down a tiny tube into your small intestine. Your **pancreas** is another part of your body that helps you digest food. Juices made by your pancreas also pour into your small intestine.

These liver cells make bile to help digest fatty foods.

Amazing!

Your liver weighs about 3 pounds (1.5 kilograms). That's about the same as ten apples.

Water Waste

Thirst is your body's way of telling you that it needs something to drink. Your body needs lots of water to make it work properly. Sometimes, you take in more water than your body can use. That makes you go to the bathroom to get rid of the extra water.

Urine is stored in your **bladder**. Your bladder can hold about two big glasses of liquid.

Your **kidneys** work like tiny filters to clean your blood of any liquid waste. Urine is the yellow waste liquid made by your kidneys. The urine trickles down two tubes into a small bag called your bladder. Your bladder stretches like a balloon as it fills up with urine. A tight muscle around your bladder stops urine from seeping out. When you go to the toilet, the muscle loosens and lets the urine flow down and out of your body through another tube.

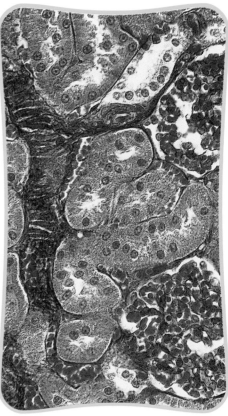

Kidney cells like these work to filter waste liquids from your blood.

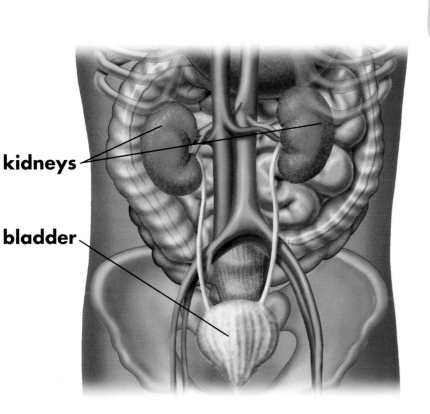

kidneys

bladder

Amazing!

In your lifetime, you make enough urine to fill about 500 bathtubs.

21

Healthy Eating

Different kinds of food do different jobs in your body. You need to eat a good mixture of different kinds of food to stay healthy. This is called eating a balanced **diet**.

Foods such as meat, fish, and beans make you grow. They also help repair worn-out parts of your body. Bread, rice, pasta, and potatoes give you energy. Fruits and vegetables are full of vitamins and minerals that keep you healthy. Milk, cheese, and yogurt make your bones and teeth strong.

Which of these meals do you think is better for you: a hot dog and fries or chicken, rice, and vegetables?

Part of this **blood vessel** is blocked with fat.

Your body also needs food that has **fiber** in it, such as corn on the cob or whole wheat bread. Fiber helps food move through your body.

Fatty foods, such as cheeses and meats, and some sweet foods give you energy, but eating too much fat is bad for you. The extra fat that you eat can build up in your blood vessels and slow or stop blood from flowing to your heart.

Amazing!

Carrots contain vitamin A, which helps your eyes see better in dim light.

Using Energy

The different kinds of food you eat give you different amounts of energy. The amount of energy in food is measured in **calories**. Sweet foods, fatty foods, meat, and dairy products have more calories than vegetables and fruits. The food you buy from a store has labels telling you how many calories are in your food.

Amazing!

Your body gets more energy from food with lots of calories, such as pizza, than from food with few calories, such as lettuce.

Do you like swimming? You burn about 600 calories an hour when you swim.

Your body is always burning calories no matter what you are doing. Sleeping uses fewer calories per hour than running, biking, or swimming. Exercise is good for you because it keeps your body fit and strong. Eating too many calories without exercising can make you overweight, which is bad for your health.

Activity

Your digestive system has different parts. How many parts can you name? Photocopy page 27 and match the numbers below to the body parts listed on page 27.

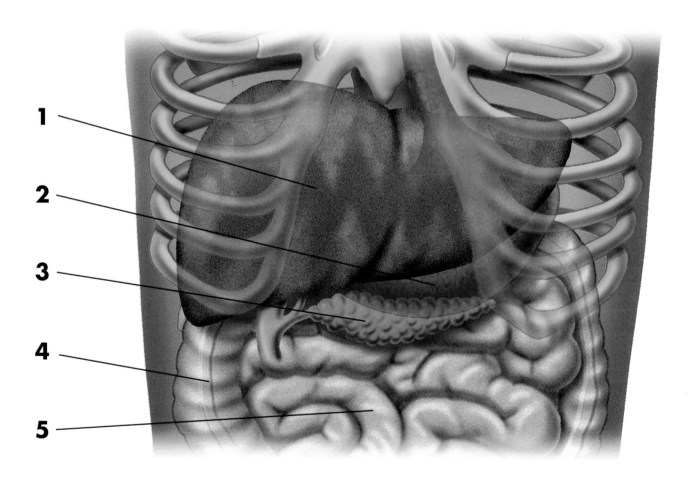

1

2

3

4

5

Do not write on this page! Ask an adult to help you photocopy this page, then write your answers on the photocopy. (See page 18 to check your answers.)

_____ **liver**

_____ **small intestine**

_____ **stomach**

_____ **pancreas**

_____ **large intestine**

Glossary

bile: a juice made by your liver that helps your body break down fats.

bladder: a "bag" that stores your urine.

blood vessel: a soft, flexible "tube" that carries blood to every area of your body.

calories: the amount of energy your body gets from using up the food you eat.

choke: to cough or gasp for breath.

cramp: sharp pains you feel when a muscle suddenly squeezes very tight.

diet: the food you eat.

digestion: the process that breaks down your food into pieces tiny enough to pass into your blood.

enamel: the hardest substance in your body. It coats the outsides of your teeth.

energy: the power that lets something move or do work.

esophagus: the muscular food tube that leads from your mouth to your stomach.

fiber: tiny strings of plant material in your food.

gall bladder: a little "bag" near your liver that stores bile.

germs: tiny living things that cause some illnesses.

hunger: an unpleasant feeling caused by muscle movements of an empty stomach.

kidneys: two body parts that clean poisons out of your blood and produce a yellow liquid called urine.

large intestine: the widest part of your food tube that stores waste.

liver: a body part that stores nutrients from your food and also cleans poisons from it.

minerals: a part of your food that keeps your body strong.

nerves: special cells that carry messages between your body and your brain. They look like very tiny wires or threads.

nutrients: tiny pieces of food that are carried around your body by your blood.

pancreas: a body part that makes several different liquids that help your body break down your food.

poisons: elements in your food or drink that cause harm, illness, or death.

saliva: a watery spit made in your mouth that helps you digest your food.

small intestine: the narrowest part of your food tube where most digestion happens.

stomach: a stretchy bag of muscles that mashes your food into smaller pieces.

taste buds: special nerve cells on your tongue that help you taste different flavors.

thirst: the feeling you get when your body needs water.

urine: the liquid you pass when you go to the bathroom.

vitamins: a part of your food that keeps your body strong.

windpipe: the main tube leading down your throat and into your lungs.

More Books to Read

Eating. Body Books (series).
  Anna Sandeman
  (Copper Beech Books)

*I Have a Weird Brother Who
  Digested a Fly.* Joan Holub
  (Albert Whitman & Co.)

*I Know Where My Food Goes.
  Sam's Science* (series).
  Jacqui Maynard
  (Candlewick Press)

*What Happens to a Hamburger?
  Let's-Read-and-Find-Out
  Science* (series).
  Paul Showers (HarperCollins)

*Why Does My Tummy Rumble
  When I'm Hungry? And Other
  Questions about the Digestive
  System. Body Wise* (series).
  Sharon Cromwell
  (Heinemann Library)

Videos

*Digestion — Food to Energy.
  Human Body Systems* (series).
  (A-Barr)

*The Human Body: Major Systems
  and Organs. Just the Facts*
  (series). (Goldhil Media)

Web Sites

BrainPOP: Digestive System.
  www.brainpop.com/health/
  digestive/

*How the Body Works: Digestive
  System.* kidshealth.org/misc_
  pages/bodyworks/digest.html

Index